SUPREME COURT CASES

THROUGH PRIMARY SOURCES™

Plessy  v. Ferguson

Legalizing Segregation

Wayne Anderson

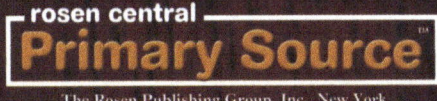

To my siblings, Denise, Mark, Marsha, Everold, and Kevin

Published in 2004 by The Rosen Publishing Group, Inc.
29 East 21st Street, New York, NY 10010

Copyright © 2004 by The Rosen Publishing Group, Inc.

First Edition

All rights reserved. No part of this book may be reproduced in any form without permission in writing from the publisher, except by a reviewer.

Unless otherwise attributed, all quotes in this book are excerpted from court transcripts.

Library of Congress Cataloging-in-Publication Data

Anderson, Wayne, 1966–
Plessy v. Ferguson: legalizing segregation / by Wayne Anderson.
   p. cm. — (Supreme Court cases through primary sources)
Includes bibliographical references and index.
ISBN: 978-1-4358-3647-1
1. Plessy, Homer Adolph—Trials, litigation, etc. 2. Segregation in transportation—Law and legislation—Louisiana—History.
3. Segregation—Law and legislation—United States—History. 4. United States—Race relations—History. I. Title: Plessy vs Ferguson. II. Title: Plessy versus Ferguson. III. Title. IV. S547eries.
KF223.P56 A53 2003
342.73'0873—dc21

2002154574

Manufactured in the United States of America

Contents

Introduction 4
1. **The Social Environment** 7
2. **A Ride into History** 17
3. **The Case for Plessy** 24
4. **The Case for Louisiana** 33
5. **The Decision** 39
6. **The Aftermath** 50

Glossary 55
For More Information 57
For Further Reading 58
Bibliography 59
Primary Source Image List 60
Index 61

Introduction

The United States Supreme Court plays a special role in the United States's system of government. As the highest judicial body in the nation, it has the power to check the actions of the president, Congress, and state governments. In other words, the Supreme Court can overrule any law passed by Congress and state legislatures and can set aside any policy adopted by the president if it determines that the law or policy breaks a rule of the U.S. Constitution.

The Supreme Court has the final say in all cases involving the Constitution. Once the Supreme Court rules on an issue, the president, Congress, all state and local governments, and all other courts are expected to follow its lead. Consequently, its decisions have significant influence on public policy. It is therefore no surprise that people who believe that a law or policy denies them a constitutional right

Introduction

Although the Supreme Court Building was not completed until 1935, the motto running across its facade—Equal Justice Under Law—has long been a cornerstone of American legal theory, stretching back to the founding fathers. However, African Americans have not always been provided equal justice by the Court.

often begin legal battles with the hope that their case will eventually be heard by the Supreme Court.

In 1892, a small group of black professionals in New Orleans, Louisiana, challenged the constitutionality of a Louisiana law that ordered separate accommodations for blacks and whites on railroads that operated wholly within the state. In a carefully planned effort, a fair-skinned black man named Homer Plessy was arrested after he refused to give up the seat he had taken in a car reserved for whites.

Plessy v. Ferguson

The group sponsored his case throughout the legal system all the way to the United States Supreme Court. In 1896, in one of its most criticized and controversial decisions, the Supreme Court ruled in the case of *Plessy v. Ferguson* that the law was constitutional. The Court said that it was acceptable for a state to order racial segregation (separation of blacks and whites) in public facilities as long as the facilities assigned to blacks were equal to those reserved for whites. The decision provided legal justification for forced segregation in almost all aspects of public life throughout the United States, though primarily in the South, until it was overturned by the Supreme Court fifty-eight years later.

The Social Environment

1

The challenge to the Louisiana law that led to the *Plessy v. Ferguson* decision was one of many efforts by African Americans throughout the United States to claim rights they were supposed to have gained from the Emancipation Proclamation of 1863 and several new amendments to the Constitution that followed the proclamation. These rights came after a long and bitter struggle over the position of blacks in American society. However, blacks soon found out that securing those rights for themselves would require another struggle in the face of deep-seated resentment.

SLAVERY

From the mid-seventeenth century to 1865, the majority of the black residents of the United States lived in the South as slaves. Their labor supported a farming industry, dominated

Plessy v. Ferguson

Based on an 1864 painting by David G. Blythe, this lithograph portrays President Abraham Lincoln writing the Emancipation Proclamation. It shows Lincoln with a Bible and a copy of the Constitution in his lap, two of his greatest sources of moral inspiration. Although widely regarded as the document that ended slavery in the United States, the Emancipation Proclamation applied only to slaves in the Confederate states over which the federal government did not have control. The lithograph is part of the collection of the Library of Congress Prints and Photographs Division.

by the production of cotton, that was the mainstay of the southern economy and a significant contributor to the economy of the United States as a whole. As slaves, blacks had no rights. They were regarded not as people, but as property. As such, their treatment depended on the slaveholders. They had little say in the decisions regarding their welfare.

Over time, opposition to slavery grew beyond the efforts of slaves trying to escape to freedom and a loose movement of

The Social Environment

people mainly in the North, known as abolitionists, agitating for an immediate end to slavery. By the late 1820s, the influence of the abolitionists had become so strong that an end to slavery was the apparent goal of the states in the North. This development led to increasing tensions between the North (dominated by Republicans, who were overwhelmingly pro-abolition) and the South (controlled by Democrats, who were mostly pro-slavery) that would eventually explode into the bloodiest conflict in U.S. history, the American Civil War.

CIVIL WAR

The 1860 presidential election campaign was extremely controversial and focused almost exclusively on slavery. Within months after the election of Republican Abraham Lincoln, who had argued against the spread of slavery, eleven southern states, including Louisiana, seceded from the United States and joined forces to create a separate nation, called the Confederate States of America. Confederate forces attacked federal troops at Fort Sumter near Charleston, South Carolina, on April 12, 1861, thereby beginning the Civil War.

The Civil War lasted four years, and during its span, approximately 179,000 African Americans served in the Union (Northern) army. Before the war was over, President Lincoln issued the Emancipation Proclamation as a military order that freed the slaves in the Confederate states. He also pushed Congress to approve the Thirteenth Amendment to the Constitution, which banned slavery throughout the United States.

Plessy v. Ferguson

This 1864 photograph, part of the Library of Congress's collection of Civil War images, shows black soldiers standing in uniform behind white Union officers at Brandy Station, Virginia, during the Civil War. Although more than 3,000 black soldiers died from battle wounds, their participation in the war helped destroy slavery.

The Civil War officially ended when Confederate general Robert E. Lee surrendered on April 9, 1865. With the defeat of the Confederacy, the former slaves were forced to face the realities of freedom, including the challenge of finding food and shelter. Some worked out agreements with their former masters to continue to work on the cotton fields in exchange for wages, food, and shelter. However, they worked under conditions similar to those that existed under slavery. Others moved away to cities in the North in search of work, education, and relief offered by charitable organizations. But

The Social Environment

for the vast majority of the newly freed slaves, called freedmen, there was the prospect of desolation and starvation. To counter this, Congress established the Freedmen's Bureau, which helped blacks, and even poor whites, find jobs and obtain an education.

RECONSTRUCTION

Despite losing the Civil War and notwithstanding the ratification (approval) of the Thirteenth Amendment in 1865, the former Confederate states passed a set of laws known as the black codes to restore as many of the features of the former slave system as possible. With these laws, the South's leaders tried to regulate the movements and activities of blacks. Outraged by these laws, Congress, led by Republicans from the North, moved quickly to pass a civil rights act, the Fourteenth and Fifteenth Amendments, and the Reconstruction acts, which guaranteed basic civil rights to blacks, including the right to vote for black males.

The Reconstruction acts passed by Congress in 1867 and 1868, which outlined a program for rebuilding the economy of the South and bringing the former Confederate states back into the United States, were harsher than Lincoln and his successor, Andrew Johnson, had intended. Because of this, the program—and the period in which it occurred—is known as the Radical Reconstruction. During the Radical Reconstruction, the South was divided into five military districts supported by federal troops. Each district was headed by a commander from the North whose responsibilities included overseeing the writing of new state constitutions and supervising elections to set up new

Plessy v. Ferguson

state governments. Each of the states had to ratify the Thirteenth and Fourteenth Amendments to be readmitted into the Union. The new state governments that developed under Reconstruction ratified the three new amendments, including the Fifteenth Amendment, which gave black men the right to vote.

Black life was much improved under Reconstruction. The most common example of this was found in how much blacks moved around. After years of having their movements restricted by slave owners, ex-slaves took advantage of their newfound freedom of movement to search for long-lost family members and for better opportunities elsewhere. With the right to vote, many blacks were elected to local and state government offices. Some even served in Congress. These officeholders worked hard to improve the lives of the people they represented and to achieve equality between the races. As a result, many public facilities were integrated and others, such as schools, were founded to cater to freedpeople and poor whites. Blacks also established other institutions, especially churches, which served as social and political centers for their communities.

Southern whites regarded the period of Reconstruction with great resentment. Former Confederates were bitter about losing the war, which devastated the Southern economy. They did not like to see their state governments, from which they were excluded, being run by a coalition of invaders from the North, whom they called carpetbaggers, and blacks.

In short order, the most ardent objectors to Reconstruction began efforts to deny blacks their civil rights

The Social Environment

This 1872 portrait shows the first group of black congressmen in United States history. The men came to office during Reconstruction, when black men first gained the right to vote. In all, sixteen blacks served in the House of Representatives and the Senate during Reconstruction.

and, more important, to regain control of the South. Their methods included appealing to white voters to vote for the Democrats; threatening to fire blacks who voted for the Republicans, if they tried to vote; and carrying out a reign of terror against blacks through violent, extremist organizations, such as the Ku Klux Klan. Klan members, who usually operated at night and were often led by some of the most prominent members of the community, attacked blacks and their white supporters—threatening, beating, burning, and killing them, as well as burning their homes and churches.

Plessy v. Ferguson

JIM CROW

State by state, southern Democrats took control of the local governments and within a few years reemerged as a formidable force with which Republicans had to reckon. By 1873, congressional zeal to both rebuild the South and address the plight of black people began to waver as Republicans turned their attention to a faltering national economy. This change in focus only strengthened the hands of the southern Democrats, who forced the Republicans into a political compromise in 1877 that ended Reconstruction. Even before the federal troops were pulled out of the South, many southern state and local governments began reinstating the black codes. Within a decade, laws enforcing segregation were the order of the day in most southern states. These laws were known as Jim Crow laws.

Louisiana was among the last of the southern states to adopt these segregation laws. This may have been a reflection of the fact that Louisiana blacks were the most prosperous and politically active in the South—perhaps because there was a large population of freedmen in the state even before the Civil War. However, in 1890, over the objection of the eighteen black assembly members, the Louisiana state legislature passed the Separate Car Act, mandating "separate but equal" accommodations for blacks and whites on all intrastate (in-state) passenger railways, except street railroads. The law stated that, except for nurses attending the children of another race, no person "shall be permitted to occupy seats in coaches, other than the ones assigned to them, on account of the race they belonged to." It required train officers to assign passengers to cars based on race

The Social Environment

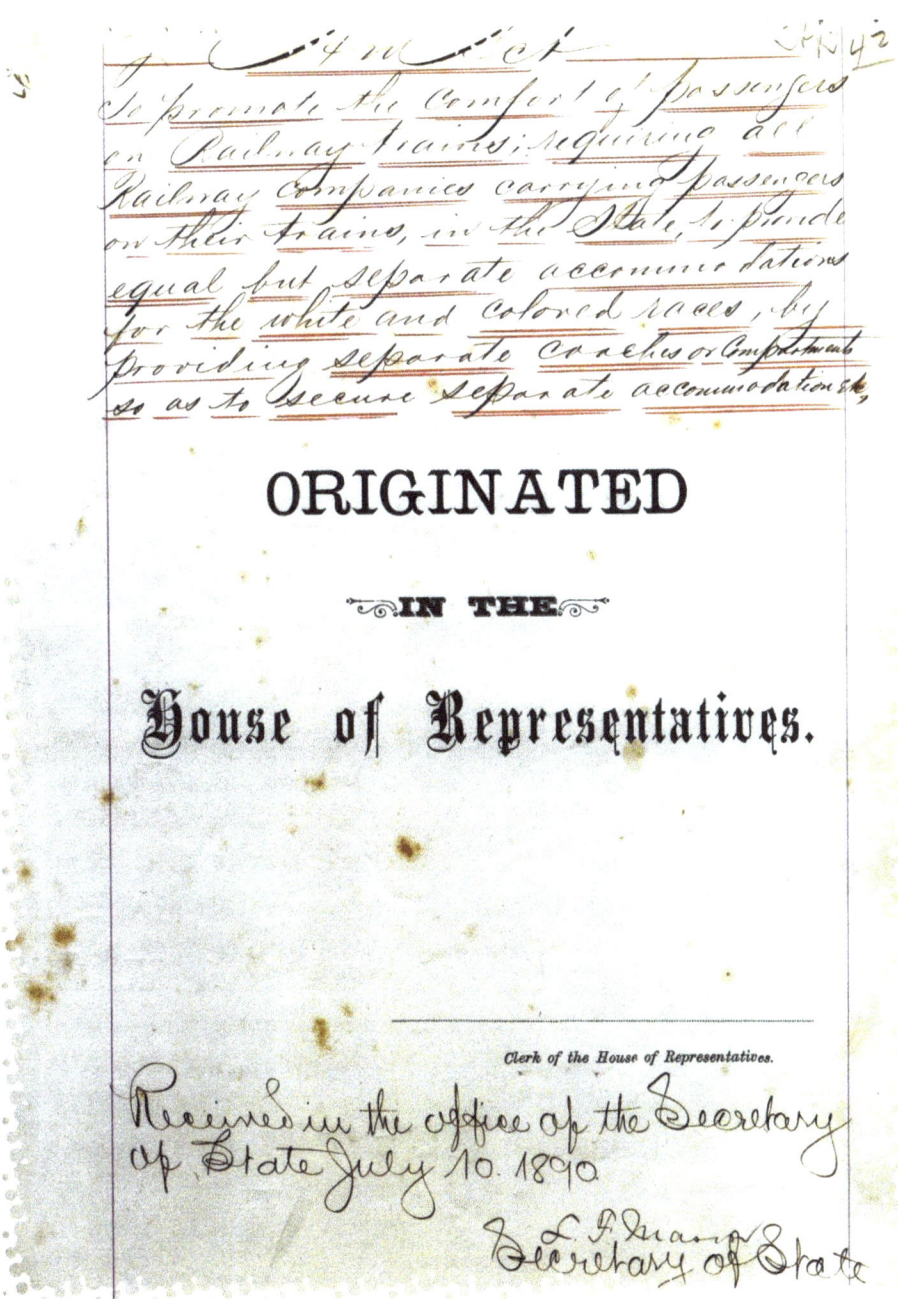

This is a copy of a page—quite likely the cover sheet—from Louisiana's 1890 Separate Car Act. Written at the top of the page is a statement describing the purpose of the law as "promoting the comfort of passengers in railway trains."

Plessy v. Ferguson

and carried a $25 fine or twenty-day jail term for conductors who made an incorrect assignment and for passengers who insisted on going into a coach in which they didn't belong. The law also gave train officers the power to refuse to carry a passenger who didn't cooperate with a proper assignment.

New Orleans's leading black residents immediately denounced the law and threatened to challenge it in courts. The following year, a number of black professionals formed the Citizens' Committee to Test the Constitutionality of the Separate Car Law. The Citizens' Committee appointed Albion Tourgée, a successful white lawyer and novelist who had previously fought for the rights of African Americans, to head its legal team, which included James C. Walker, a white lawyer who had strong political ties to Republican politics in Louisiana, and Louis Martinet, a member of the Citizens' Committee. Under Tourgée's guidance, the committee developed a strategy to purposefully break the law in order to chart a course toward getting a hearing before the United States Supreme Court. A thirty-year-old shoemaker named Homer Plessy agreed to be the guinea pig to challenge the law.

A Ride into History

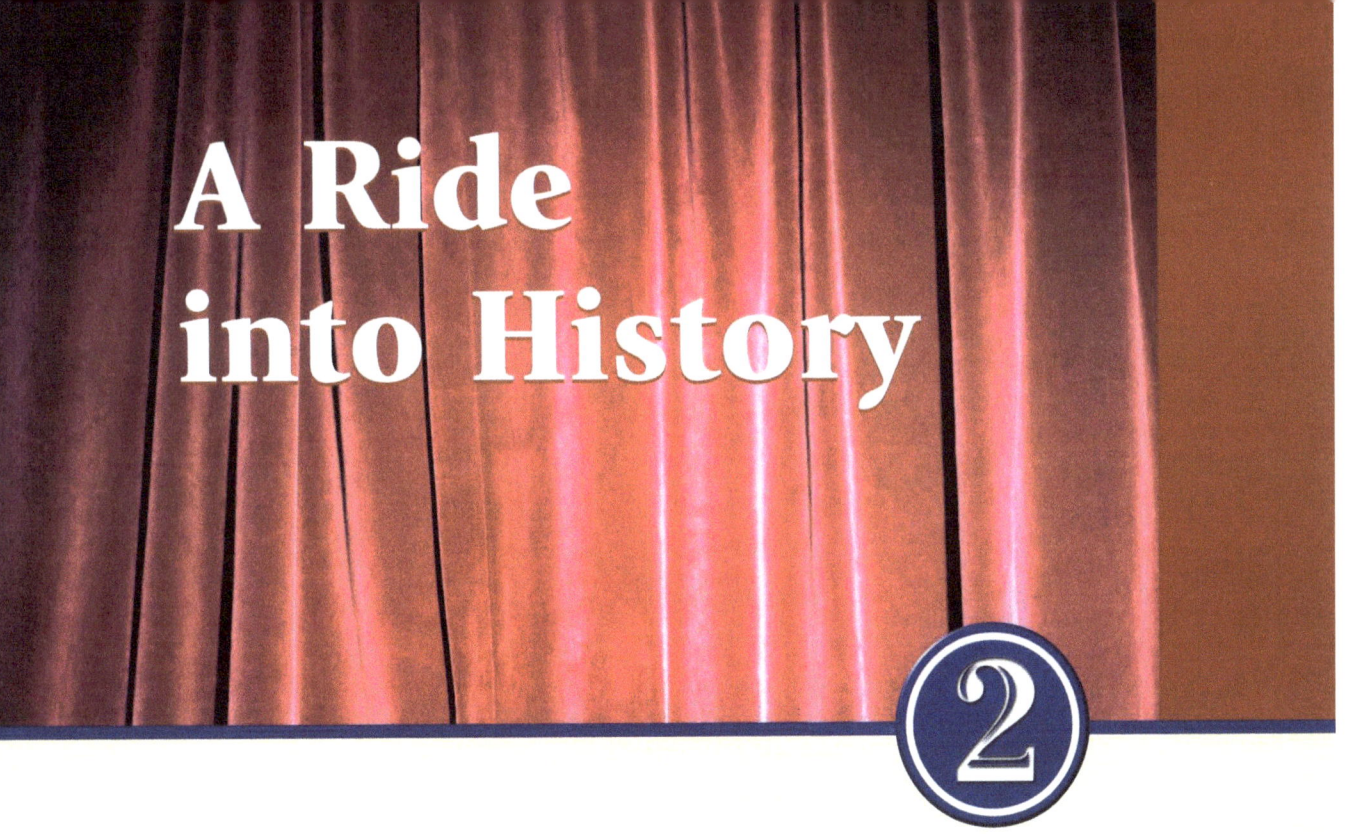

On June 7, 1892, Homer Plessy bought a first-class ticket to Covington, Louisiana, on the East Louisiana Railroad. The railroad operated entirely within the state of Louisiana. Plessy boarded the train in New Orleans and took a seat in the car designated for white passengers. He didn't seem to be out of place, because although he was considered a black man by law, he looked like a white man. In fact, Plessy was only one-eighth black, which means that one of his eight great-grandparents was black. When the conductor came to collect his ticket, he asked Plessy to move to the "black" car. When Plessy refused to move, the conductor had him detained by a private detective.

How did the conductor know that Plessy was riding in the wrong car? The whole scene had been arranged between the Citizens' Committee, the detective, and the

Plessy v. Ferguson

This is a photo of an advertisement for the East Louisiana Railroad Company, circa 1900. Homer Plessy was arrested for attempting to ride in one of the railway's whites-only cars in 1892. The photo is part of the Historic New Orleans Collection.

railroad, which did not like the new law because of the additional expenses of providing separate cars for the two races. The detective took Plessy to a police station, where Plessy was booked and released on a $500 bond paid by a member of the Citizens' Committee.

PLESSY FACES A CRIMINAL TRIAL

A month later, Assistant District Attorney Lionel Adams filed charges against Plessy, and Plessy was arraigned, or called to court to answer the charges against him, in a

A Ride into History

WHO WAS HOMER PLESSY?

When Homer Plessy entered the first-class "white" railroad car in New Orleans on June 7, 1892, he was going nowhere in particular. But his brave step in protest of an unfair law assured him a place in history, despite his eventual retreat into anonymity. We know very little about the man at the center of one of the most influential and infamous cases in American history. There are no photographs of him, and except for court records that describe him as being light-skinned enough to pass for white, we know nothing of what he looked like. The public details of his life present only a sketch.

Plessy was born on March 17, 1862, the second child of Adolphe Plessy and Rosa Debergue Plessy. His father died when he was five years old, and his mother remarried shortly afterward. Plessy learned the shoemaking craft as an apprentice during his teenage years. He married Louise Bordenave in 1887. After his brush with history, he returned to a quiet life and eventually worked as a life insurance collector. Plessy died in 1925.

Louisiana district court on October 31. This was a criminal trial in which Plessy, the defendant, would face a $25 fine or a twenty-day jail sentence if he was found guilty. The presiding judge was Justice John Howard Ferguson, who had

{ 19 }

Plessy v. Ferguson

This is an undated photograph of Daniel F. Desdunes, the light-skinned black man whose challenge of the Separate Car Act in 1892 made segregation on interstate trains unconstitutional. Like Homer Plessy, Desdunes was only one-eighth black. The photograph is part of a collection at the Amistad Research Center at Tulane University.

recently decided that a law requiring segregation on interstate (between states) railroads was unconstitutional. Plessy's lawyers immediately filed a plea (a written response to the charges), which argued that the law was unconstitutional—it violated the Thirteenth and Fourteenth Amendments of the Constitution, in particular—and questioned whether Ferguson, a state judge, had the authority to hear the case.

After hearing arguments from the prosecution, led by Adams, and the defense on the plea, the judge decided that the law was constitutional and that, because of this, he was authorized to hear the case. Ferguson ruled that the state had the power to regulate railroads that operated completely within its borders.

This decision signaled the judge's intention to find Plessy guilty. But before the trial proceeded any further, Plessy's lawyers filed a writ of prohibition and petitioned the Louisiana Supreme Court to stop the trial judge from continuing the trial. The state supreme court issued a provisional, or temporary, writ of prohibition on November 22, 1892, and

A Ride into History

This is a copy of the court order issued by the Louisiana Supreme Court to Judge John Ferguson that halted the district court proceedings against Homer Plessy in 1892. The order was signed by Chief Justice Francis Nicholls, who, as governor of Louisiana in 1890, had signed the disputed Separate Car Act into law.

Plessy v. Ferguson

INSIDE THE SUPREME COURT: CASES HEARD BY THE COURT

At the time of *Plessy v. Ferguson*, the Supreme Court was obligated to accept all appeals that came to it. The caseload was particularly stressful for the justices and often clogged up the Court, causing many cases to be delayed for years. In 1925, Congress passed the Judiciary Act, which allowed the court to select the cases it wanted to hear.

Of the more than 5,000 requests for appeals submitted to the Supreme Court each year, only about 100 are heard by the justices. Cases that are eventually heard must meet the following criteria:

- Someone must have been wronged or must have a personal stake in the case.
- The appeal must be based on a constitutional claim.
- The case must involve a question of law; the Court doesn't determine if the facts presented in the lower courts are wrong.
- The plaintiff has exhausted other remedies; that is, the case has been heard by all other relevant government agencies or lower courts.

A Ride into History

ordered Judge Ferguson to give reasons why the writ should not be made permanent.

In *Ex Parte Plessy*, as the trial before the state supreme court was called (*ex parte* is Latin for "in the matter of"), the concern was not Plessy's guilt or innocence but Judge Ferguson's authority to hear the criminal case against Plessy and determine the constitutionality of the Separate Car Act. In this trial, Plessy was the plaintiff because he was the one making the charges—against Judge Ferguson. A defeat for Plessy would mean that he would have to return to the criminal court to be tried. The state supreme court eventually agreed with Judge Ferguson that the law was constitutional.

Although the state supreme court decision went against Plessy, his lawyers were pleased with the result. It was their intention all along to take the case to the U.S. Supreme Court, and they needed this unfavorable ruling to do so. On January 5, 1893, Plessy appealed the Louisiana Supreme Court ruling to the U.S. Supreme Court by filing a writ of error. Judge Ferguson was named in the case (*Plessy v. Ferguson*) because Plessy was complaining against Ferguson and his original ruling. In truth, however, the case was between Plessy and the state of Louisiana, which had passed the law in question. The case would not be heard for another three years.

The Case for Plessy

3

Now that they had an appointment with the Supreme Court, the Citizens' Committee, represented by Plessy's lawyers, had to present their case. Three lawyers would represent Plessy before the Court: Tourgée, Walker, and Samuel F. Phillips, a Washington, DC, lawyer, who was a friend of Tourgée's and a former United States solicitor general. As the lawyers for the plaintiff, they had the burden of proof. In other words, it was up to them to prove the law unconstitutional. Laws are considered to be constitutional until proven otherwise.

CHALLENGES FOR THE PLAINTIFF

The task before Plessy's lawyers was not easy. In addition to having the burden of proof, they faced a number of

The Case for Plessy

obstacles, not least of which was the continuing shift in the national mood. Since the end of Reconstruction, support for African Americans' civil rights seemed to take a backseat to meeting the demands of white southerners in order to strengthen the country. Two challenges, however, stood above the others in making the task daunting for Plessy's legal team.

First, there were few precedents, or prior court decisions, that supported Plessy's positions. In fact, the recent trend in the federal courts, including the U.S. Supreme Court, was toward narrowly defining the civil rights promised to African Americans by the Thirteenth, Fourteenth, and Fifteenth Amendments, which are known collectively as the Civil Rights Amendments. Consequently, it was easier to find precedents countering Plessy's claims than those favoring them. This was especially crucial because Supreme Court justices expect lawyers to present precedents in their arguments. Although the Court is not bound by precedents, even its own, the justices place great value on them.

Albion Winegar Tourgée was one of the leading white activists in support of civil rights for African Americans in the late nineteenth century. He represented Homer Plessy in the Supreme Court and lower court cases free of charge. This undated photo of Tourgée is archived by the Chautaugua County Historical Society in New York.

Plessy v. Ferguson

The second challenge was that the collective record of the Supreme Court justices suggested there would be little sympathy for Plessy's arguments. Tourgée pointed this out to Walker in a letter. As quoted by Charles A. Lofgren in *The Plessy Case: A Legal-Historical Interpretation*, Tourgée wrote, "Of the whole number of Justices there is but one who is known to favor the view we must stand upon." He identified four others whom he thought could be swayed by powerful arguments or public opinion even though they were inclined to vote against Plessy. He thought the remaining four were so fixed in their views that they could never be persuaded. With such a dire view of the chances of convincing the Court to rule for Plessy, Tourgée had reversed himself from an earlier decision to try to press for an early hearing. He hoped that the passing of time would lead to a more favorable Court. However, it was almost the same lineup of justices to which Tourgée referred in the letter that Plessy's legal team would face on April 13, 1896.

ARGUMENTS FOR PLESSY

Although the lawyers for both parties appear before the Supreme Court for a hearing, most of the arguments are made in briefs, written arguments detailing the law and the facts involved in the case. In fact, in a typical case, each side is allotted only thirty minutes for an oral presentation, during which the judges often interrupt to ask questions. Plessy's lawyers filed two briefs, one by Tourgée and Walker and the other by Phillips.

As noted earlier, the constitutional rights that Plessy claimed had been violated by his arrest under Louisiana's

The Case for Plessy

This is a copy of the joint resolution of the Senate and House of Representatives, passed on February 1, 1865, that proposed the Thirteenth Amendment, prohibiting slavery. The amendment was ratified by the states in December of the same year.

Plessy v. Ferguson

This engraving, published in the Illustrated London News in September 1856, depicts a white man, presumably a train conductor, ordering a freed black man to leave a whites-only car in Philadelphia. There were many dedicated abolitionists in England who fought against slavery and segregation in the United States.

Separate Car Act were those granted by the Thirteenth and Fourteenth Amendments. In order to understand Plessy's arguments, it is important to first look at the amendments.

Ratified in 1865, the Thirteenth Amendment abolished slavery throughout the United States. It reads in part: "Neither slavery nor involuntary servitude except as punishment for crime whereof the party shall have been duly convicted, shall exist within the United States, or any place subject to their jurisdiction."

Tourgée argued that this amendment was intended to not only end the institution of slavery, but also to outlaw "conditions of subjection and [forced] inferiority" that were associated with slavery. He reasoned that by sorting people by race, the Louisiana law, which he described as "a legalization of caste" (social classes people are born into), was in effect continuing an essential feature of slavery.

Most of Plessy's claims were tied to Section 1 of the Fourteenth Amendment, which was ratified in 1868. In summary, the amendment requires the government and its laws to treat all citizens equally. Section 1 reads:

The Case for Plessy

All persons born or naturalized in the United States, and subject to the jurisdiction thereof, are citizens of the United States and of the State wherein they reside. No State shall make or enforce any law which shall abridge the privileges or immunities of citizens of the United States; nor shall any State deprive any person in life, liberty, or property, without due process of law, nor deny to any person within its jurisdiction the equal protection of the laws.

Together, the two briefs filed by Plessy's lawyers attempted to show that the Louisiana law violated the Fourteenth Amendment with respect to its guarantees of equal protection, due process of the law, and the privileges and immunities of United States citizens. They identified the following equal protection violations:

- By exempting the railway and its officers from civil liability for enforcing the law, Louisiana deprived a person of the right to sue the railway for damages if he or she had been wrongly expelled from the train.
- Although the law required equal accommodations for blacks and whites, that was not the case in practice. Yet passengers faced criminal penalties for refusing to accept a seat, even if the assigned car was inferior.
- The exemption for nurses attending the other race showed that the real intention of the law was to ensure the comforts of whites at the expense of blacks. On this point, Tourgée declared, "Justice is pictured as blind and her daughter, the Law, ought at least to be color-blind."

Plessy v. Ferguson

The idea of "due process" concerns the fairness of laws, in terms of how and why they are enforced. It is a broad concept that is not very well defined. However, it entails such guarantees as clearly written laws that are applied fairly to all, a right to a fair and competent trial with an impartial jury, and the right to be present at the trial and to be heard in one's defense. Tourgée and company raised the following due process objections to the Separate Car Act:

- The law was vague in its definition of race, yet it gave the conductor the power to make the final decision regarding a person's race. Because racial mixing was so prevalent, this decision would often be guesswork and could therefore not be equitable.
- The reputation of belonging to a race was a form of property, and by allowing the conductor to make the final determination of race and to assign Plessy to the "black" car, the law deprived the white-skinned Plessy of his reputation as a white man and took away his "property."
- Allowing the conductor to refuse to carry a passenger who rejects the seat assignment denies the passenger not only access to the place he or she had a right to occupy, but also deprives the passenger of the property of the ticket he or she had purchased.
- The law interfered with the rights of parents and children of mixed marriages to travel together. Tourgée outlined a situation in which a white man could travel with his black nurse in the "white" car, while his black wife, and legally "black" kids were forced to ride in the "black" car.

The Case for Plessy

This photograph shows a group of slaves who were freed during the Civil War. It also reflects the wide range of complexions—from dark to white-skinned—among children born to black and white parents. Homer Plessy's lawyers argued that the law could not be applied fairly because conductors were often forced to guess the race of some railroad passengers.

In his brief, Tourgée pointed out that the Fourteenth Amendment had granted citizenship to African Americans. He argued that with this citizenship the former slaves had become equal to whites before the law in rights, privileges, and immunities. Accordingly, the state should have no business making distinctions between the races when it came to accommodations. Tourgée declared, "The question is not as to the equality of the privileges enjoyed, but the right of the State to label one citizen as white and another as colored in the common enjoyment of a public highway," as the Supreme Court had often

Plessy v. Ferguson

classified railways. He added that Louisiana's law made race the basis of a crime, since someone could be found guilty for "taking his seat and refusing to surrender it . . . while another person belonging to another race may occupy the same [seat] without fault."

While Plessy's lawyers cited a number of previous Supreme Court cases and other federal decisions in their briefs, none really solidly supported the core of their arguments. In fact, the decisions in several of the cases that they cited had unfavorable effects on civil rights. In addition, the portions of the Louisiana law against which they had the strongest, most supported arguments—the provisions exempting nurses and protecting the railways from civil liability—could easily be gutted without killing the force of the law. Given Tourgée's earlier prediction of the justices as having been unsympathetic to black civil rights claims, had his team done enough to persuade such a tough audience? It seems the plaintiff was asking a conservative court to accept a new, open-minded interpretation of the Constitution.

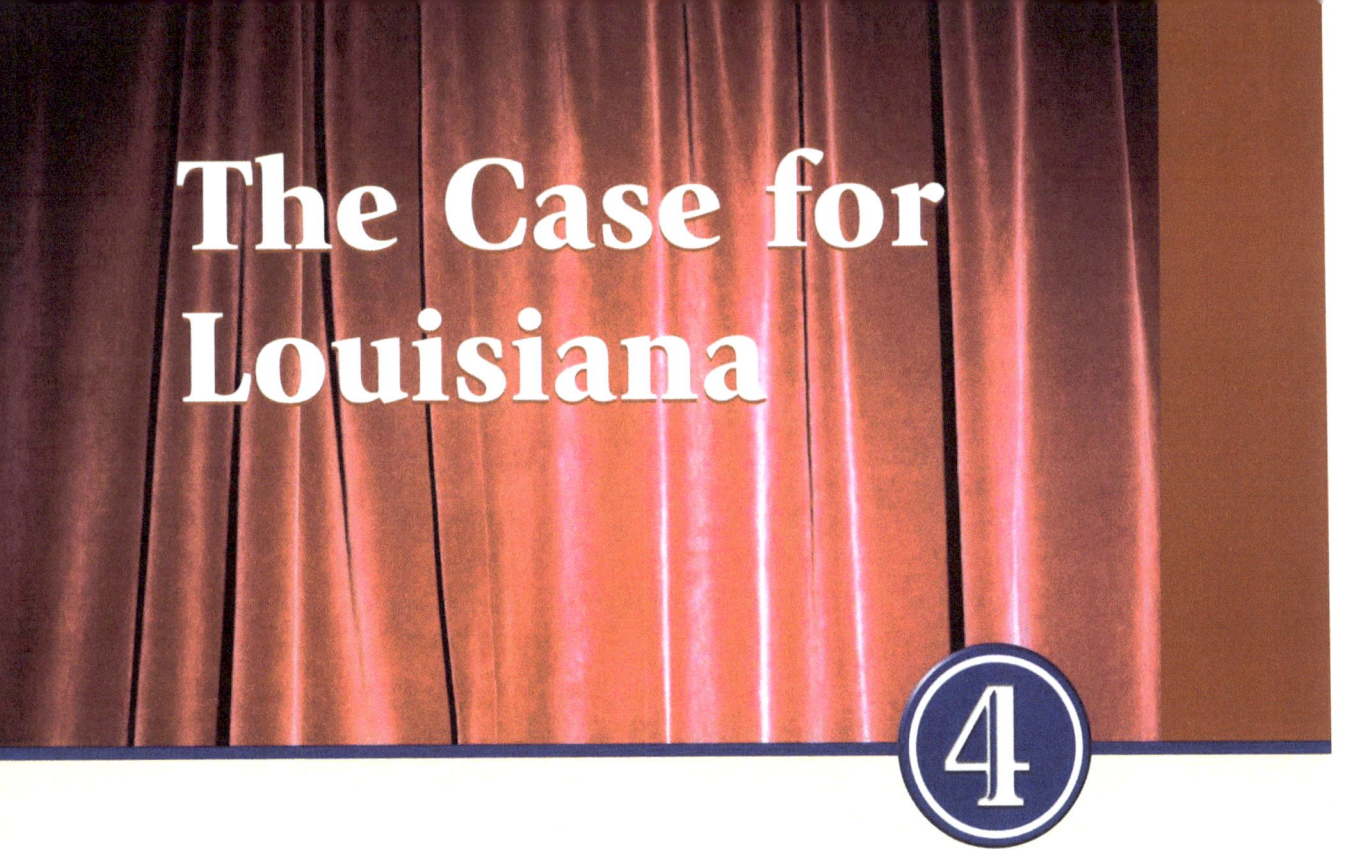

The Case for Louisiana

4

Louisiana's answer to Homer Plessy's complaint to the U.S. Supreme Court was presented in briefs by the state's attorney general, Milton J. Cunningham, and by Alexander Porter Morse, a Washington, DC, lawyer whom Cunningham had hired to help with the case. The challenges faced by Plessy's lawyers—lack of precedents, makeup of the Court, the national mood, and the racial attitudes—were, naturally, advantages for the state's case. Nevertheless, the lawyers for Louisiana still had to show why the law was within the power of the states to enact.

To meet that challenge, Louisiana relied on the Tenth Amendment to the Constitution, which says, "The powers not delegated to the United States by the Constitution, nor prohibited by it to the states, are reserved to the states respectively, or to the people." These broad, undefined powers are

Plessy v. Ferguson

often referred to as the states' "police powers," and they give states the right to create any laws that are not forbidden by the Constitution. Therefore, to show that Louisiana had the right to enact the Separate Car Act, Cunningham and Morse had to prove that the law did not violate the Constitution as Plessy claimed.

LOUISIANA'S ARGUMENTS

Cunningham compiled his brief from Assistant District Attorney Adams's brief to the Louisiana Supreme Court and the decision of that court in *Ex Parte Plessy*—both of which he carried word for word—as well as his own short discussion on the problems of classifying people by race. He defended the law as the proper use of the state's police powers to preserve the peace and health of the community. The brief repeated a claim made earlier by Adams that hostilities between the races made separating them reasonable. The document also quickly brushed aside Plessy's Thirteenth Amendment claim by declaring that denying someone accommodations in a public facility did not subject the person to any form of servitude, especially slavery.

On the question of whether Louisiana had deprived Plessy of his Fourteenth Amendment equal protection rights, Cunningham argued that the law applied equally to both races. People of both races faced the same penalties if they insisted on riding in a car to which they were not assigned. Therefore, it could not be said that the law discriminated against blacks. In support of this argument, Cunningham's

The Case for Louisiana

This photograph, part of the Historic New Orleans Collection, shows a train crew in New Orleans, Louisiana, in 1887. The state's Separate Car Act made it the crew's responsibility to enforce segregation on the trains. Louisiana's lawyers argued that it was the state's constitutional right to give this power to train crews.

brief, by way of the state supreme court ruling, also cited a number of cases in state and federal courts that upheld segregation in schools and on other public carriers, including railroads.

In its ruling in *Ex Parte Plessy*, the Louisiana Supreme Court had determined that the law did not exempt railroads and their officers from civil liability, as Plessy's lawyers had claimed, nor did it subject a person who refused to accept a seat that had been improperly assigned to criminal liability. These rulings undercut some of the due process and equal protection arguments that

Plessy v. Ferguson

THE TIMES-PICAYUNE, SATURDAY,

JUDGE FERGUSON, RETIRED LAWYER, DIES AT AGE OF 77

Latter Months of Life Saddened by Deaths of His Son and Wife.

Judge John Howard Ferguson died early Friday morning of cerebral hemorrhage, the result of a fall in Camp street near Canal three weeks ago, when his head struck the pavement with force. Although Judge Ferguson had reached the age of 77 years, and had retired from the active practice of law in which he had been engaged for more than half a century, his spirit was youthful, and his faculties well preserved. He was a famous as a raconteur, the personification of geniality, but his heart was heavy long before the accident laid him low, for last June his son, Walter J. Ferguson, a prominent insurance man, died suddenly in a distant city, and three

The constitutionality of Judge John Howard Ferguson's ruling against Homer Plessy was in question in the 1896 Supreme Court case of Plessy v. Ferguson, *which explains why his name makes up part of the name of the case. This photo was published in the* New Orleans Times-Picayune *on November 13, 1915, as part of an obituary for Ferguson, who had died on the previous day.*

the plaintiff made. Cunningham also rejected Plessy's claims about the arbitrariness of the conductor's seat assignment by declaring that "every man must know the difference between a negro and a white man, [and] that the exercise of judgement is not necessary to determine the question."

Louisiana countered Tourgée's argument about reputation being a form of property with the logic that whether or not someone was deprived of such a property would depend on how the person had been assigned on the train. If the passenger was assigned to the proper car, according to his or her race, then no property was lost. If, however, the person had been assigned to the wrong car, then he or she could seek damages to recover the property lost, be it reputation or ticket. Of course, by this reasoning, a person, such as Plessy, who insists on buying a ticket for a car to which, by law, he or she does not belong bears the risk of not being able to use the ticket and can seek no damages.

The Case for Louisiana

INSIDE THE SUPREME COURT: ORAL ARGUMENTS

The Supreme Court's term for deciding cases lasts between the first Monday in October and the end of June. During that time, its schedule alternates between two weeks of open court, called sessions, when it hears oral arguments, and two weeks of recess, in which the justices read petitions and write opinions. During the weeks when the Court is in session, the justices meet on Mondays through Wednesdays from 10:00 AM to 3:00 PM with a one-hour lunch break.

Ordinary cases are allotted one hour for arguments, and the time is divided evenly between the parties. Attorneys are advised not to read from their written briefs; the justices do not approve of that. In any case, the attorneys often spend a lot of this time answering questions, posed by the justices, who often use the questions to argue with their colleagues.

MORSE'S BRIEF

In his brief on Louisiana's behalf, Alexander Morse reiterated and stressed several of the arguments addressed in the main brief. He also offered an argument that distinguished between civic rights, such as the right to vote, which were not affected by the Separate Car Act, and social rights. Pointing out that

Plessy v. Ferguson

recent federal court decisions had not viewed the Fourteenth Amendment as limiting the police powers of the states, he declared social rights to be the domain of the states, not the federal government.

In response to Plessy's claim that the "black" cars were inferior to the "white" cars, Morse and the Louisiana state supreme court argued that states were allowed to set up separate accommodations as long as they were roughly equal. In other words, the "equal" requirement doesn't mean that the cars had to be identical. Although the differences in the cars were pronounced, Louisiana felt comfortable with this interpretation.

For the most part, Louisiana ignored Plessy's arguments about citizenship and, according to Charles Lofgren, "never grappled with Albion Tourgée's challenging reading of the true meaning of the recent amendments." Nevertheless, the inclusion of the state supreme court's decision, which undermined some of Tourgée's interpretations of the law, plus the number of precedents the state's lawyers offered, added legal force to Louisiana's case.

The Decision

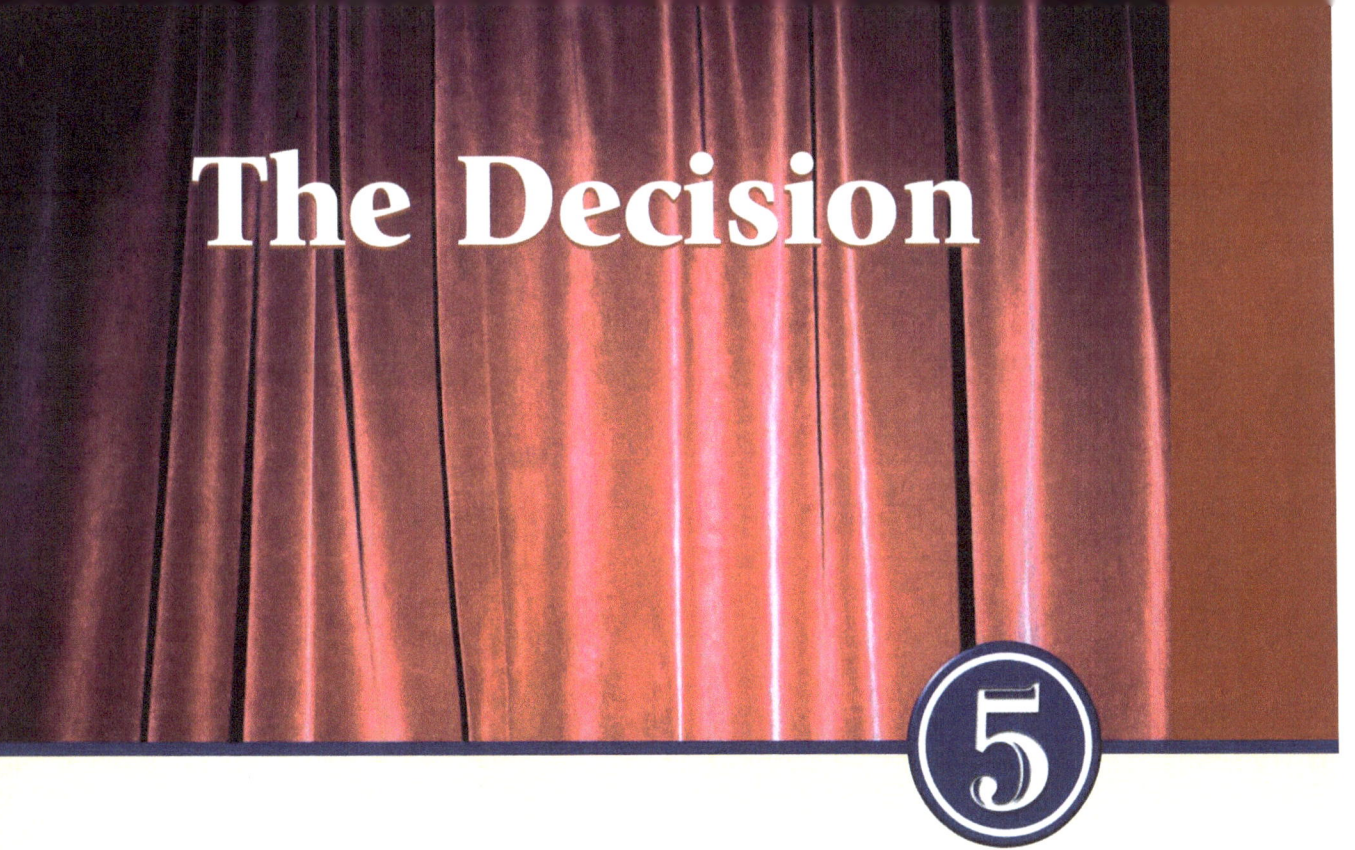

5

On May 18, 1896, the U.S. Supreme Court handed down its ruling. Eight of the nine justices participated in the decision. By a vote of 7 to 1, the Court upheld the Louisiana Separate Car Act as constitutional, with the majority opinion mirroring Louisiana's argument and the dissenting opinion (the opinion of the judge who disagreed with the others) closely reflecting Plessy's position.

THE MAJORITY OPINION

Justice Henry Billings Brown wrote the opinion for the majority. After briefly restating the facts of the case, he immediately dismissed Plessy's Thirteenth Amendment argument as "lacking constitutional conflict" before cutting apart his Fourteenth Amendment claims. To do this, Brown made a distinction between political and social equality that held

Plessy v. Ferguson

Supreme Court of the United States,

No. 210, October Term, 1895.

Homer Adolph Plessy,
Plaintiff in Error,

vs.

J. H. Ferguson, Judge of Section "A" Criminal District Court for the Parish of Orleans.

In Error to the Supreme Court of the State of Louisiana.

This cause came on to be heard on the transcript of the record from the Supreme Court of the State of Louisiana, and was argued by counsel.

On consideration whereof, It is now here ordered and adjudged by this Court that the judgment of the said Supreme Court, in this cause, be, and the same is hereby, Affirmed with costs.

Per Mr. Justice Brown,
May 18, 1896.

Dissenting:
Mr. Justice Harlan

This is a copy of the Supreme Court order affirming the Court's decision in Plessy v. Ferguson. It is noted that the document was signed by Justice Henry Brown on May 18, 1896. Justice John Marshall Harlan dissented with the majority.

The Decision

that blacks and whites were politically equal but not socially equal. He wrote:

> The object of the amendment was undoubtedly to enforce the absolute equality of the races before the law, but in the nature of things it could not have been intended to abolish distinctions based upon color, or to enforce social, as distinguished from political, equality, or a commingling of the two races upon terms unsatisfactory to either.

This is an official 1906 Supreme Court portrait of Justice Henry Billings Brown, who wrote the majority opinion in Plessy v. Ferguson. Despite his ruling in Plessy, Brown was known for his fairness. Over time, the Court's opinion has become one of the most notorious and criticized decisions in Supreme Court history.

Some historians read the phrase "in the nature of things" as Justice Brown inserting his personal bias against blacks into the decision. Others say it was simply another way of saying that segregation in public amenities was common practice within the country. In any event, neither interpretation would clash with the widely accepted views of the time. Brown did cite a number of cases, including several in liberal northern states, that allowed for segregation in schools.

{ 41 }

Plessy v. Ferguson

Justice Brown argued that the crucial issue in the case was whether the law was a reasonable use of the state's police powers. He applied to it a standard that was set in an earlier case, *Yick Wo v. Hopkins* (1886), which held that a police measure should not discriminate against one group. He did not see that shortcoming in the Louisiana law. As far as the majority was concerned, the feature of "separate but equal" made the law reasonable because it also provided "equal" accommodations for blacks.

Brown identified two fallacies, or illogical arguments, in Plessy's presentation. First he said that if the "enforced separations of the two races stamps the colored race with a badge of inferiority," as Tourgée had claimed, "it is not by reason of anything found in the act, but solely because the colored race chooses to put that construction upon it." He had bought Louisiana's argument that since people of both races were forbidden from sitting in the car assigned to the other race and both cars were, more or less, equal, then both blacks and whites were treated equally under the law.

Second was the assumption that "social prejudices may be overcome by legislation, and that equal rights cannot be secured to the negro except by an enforced commingling of the two races." Brown's characterization of Plessy's plea—that the law should protect Plessy's right against racist state legislation—offers a twist that was probably not intended by the plaintiff. Nevertheless, his response to his misread of Plessy's point is revealing. He argued, "If the civil and political rights of both races be equal, one cannot be inferior to the other civilly or politically. If one race be inferior to the other socially, the Constitution of the United States cannot put them upon the same plane." In other words, Brown was arguing that it was OK

The Decision

for a state to protect the social rights of one race with its laws, but misguided for the national government to use its laws to defend the social rights of the other race.

THE DISSENTING OPINION

Justice John Marshall Harlan wrote the dissenting opinion in *Plessy v. Ferguson*. In it, he attacked the Louisiana law as being unconstitutional and declared that the law separated the races to satisfy white racial prejudice. He wrote that while the law may appear to treat blacks and whites equally, "every one knows that the statute in question had its origin in the purpose, not so much to exclude white persons from railroad cars occupied by blacks, as to exclude colored people from coaches occupied by or assigned to white persons."

Harlan accepted Plessy's view that the Thirteenth and Fourteenth Amendments guaranteed certain essential rights for all United States citizens. He argued that, together, the amendments erased a "race line" from the United States's system of government, making the Constitution color-blind. Accordingly,

In disagreeing with the decision of his colleagues in Plessy v. Ferguson, Justice John Marshall Harlan correctly predicted the negative impact that the ruling would have on American life. However, within a couple of years, Justice Harlan began voting in favor of the type of segregation laws he so vigorously opposed in the Plessy case.

{ 43 }

Plessy v. Ferguson

he found the law to be "inconsistent with that equality of rights which pertains to citizenship, National and State."

Harlan found fault with Brown's claim that the crucial issue was the reasonableness of the law. For Harlan, the task before the Court was to determine whether the law was constitutional and not what was reasonable. The color-blind nature of the Constitution, as Harlan saw it, meant that the Supreme Court and the laws should regard "man as man" and take "no account of his surrounding or of his color when his civil rights as guaranteed by the supreme law of the land are involved." Measured against this standard, the Louisiana law was "hostile to both the spirit and the letter of the Constitution."

While making this argument, Harlan also posed the question that if states were allowed to enforce segregation in the use of public facilities by race, what would prevent them from so dividing the streets or from mandating segregation by religion, such as one car for Protestants and another for Catholics? For Harlan, everyone was entitled to hold his or her prejudices and individual sense of pride. Such considerations, however, should not enter into the acts of legislative and judicial bodies.

Finally, Harlan sounded a warning about the potential consequences of the majority's decision. He predicted that it would foster legislations that would "arouse race hate" and "perpetuate a feeling of distrust" between the races. In perhaps the most famous sentence from his opinion, he scolded the majority, declaring, "The thin disguise of 'equal' accommodations for passengers in railroad coaches will not mislead any one, nor atone for the wrong this day done."

The Decision

THE MEMBERS OF THE COURT

As Albion Tourgée indicated in his letter to James Walker, the composition of the Court can influence the outcome of the case. How a justice interprets the Constitution depends on a number of factors, including his or her own personal experiences. Reading the mood of the Court requires an understanding of who the justices are, what their philosophies are, and the record of their votes in decisions. The following is a brief description of the Supreme Court justices who were on the court during the *Plessy v. Ferguson* case.

David Josiah Brewer This fifty-nine-year-old justice was born in Asia Minor (now Turkey), the son of missionaries with strong antislavery roots. A staunch defender of the Tenth Amendment, he often advocated protecting the states from federal interference. Brewer withdrew from the hearing for undisclosed reasons. Some historians speculate that he might have felt he could not be impartial.

Henry Billings Brown The sixty-year-old justice from Massachusetts was the son of a wealthy businessman who had refused to serve in the Union army during the Civil War. Brown was an expert in maritime and patent law, and he wrote many of

continued on page 46

Plessy v. Ferguson

continued from page 45

the Court's decisions in these matters. Considered moderate to conservative, he could usually be counted on to support a state's right to assert its police powers. He wrote the majority opinion in *Plessy v. Ferguson*.

Stephen Johnson Field An eighty-year-old Democrat from Connecticut, Field was known for favoring big business in his opinions, so much so that he used the Fourteenth Amendment to assign equal protection and due process rights to corporations. However, he was reluctant to extend such considerations to African Americans and had even dissented in a number of decisions that upheld the rights of blacks to serve on juries.

Melville Weston Fuller A Democrat from Maine, Fuller did not support Lincoln or the North during the Civil War. At the time, he even backed a state constitutional amendment that denied blacks the right to vote. At sixty-three, he was the Supreme Court chief justice. He decided who wrote the opinion of the Court.

Horace Gray As a young man, Horace Gray had been a member of the Free-Soil Party, which had an antislavery platform, and had worked as a reporter to the Massachusetts judicial supreme court. He came to the Supreme Court from a distinguished career in

The Decision

private practice. He put a lot of value on precedents and was considered to have been unlikely to rule for Plessy. He was sixty-eight.

John Marshall Harlan This sixty-three-year-old former slaveholder from Kentucky had fought for the North during the Civil War and freed his slaves before the war ended. He was known as the Great Dissenter because of his frequent clashes with the majority of the Court. He was the justice whom Albert Tourgée had correctly identified as being sympathetic to Plessy's constitutional civil rights claims.

Rufus Wheeler Peckham This fifty-eight-year-old justice from Albany, New York, came to the Supreme Court following a career in corporate law. He was a strong supporter of business interests and often advocated due process rights for corporations.

George Shiras Jr. A sixty-four-year-old justice from Pittsburgh, Pennsylvania, Shiras came to the Court from private practice. His career on the bench was unspectacular, and he tended to side with the majority.

Edward Douglas White This fifty-one-year-old Roman Catholic from Louisiana joined the Confederate army during the Civil War and was captured by the Union army. He was an active Democrat in Louisiana politics after the war, and there were rumors that linked him to the Ku Klux Klan.

Plessy v. Ferguson

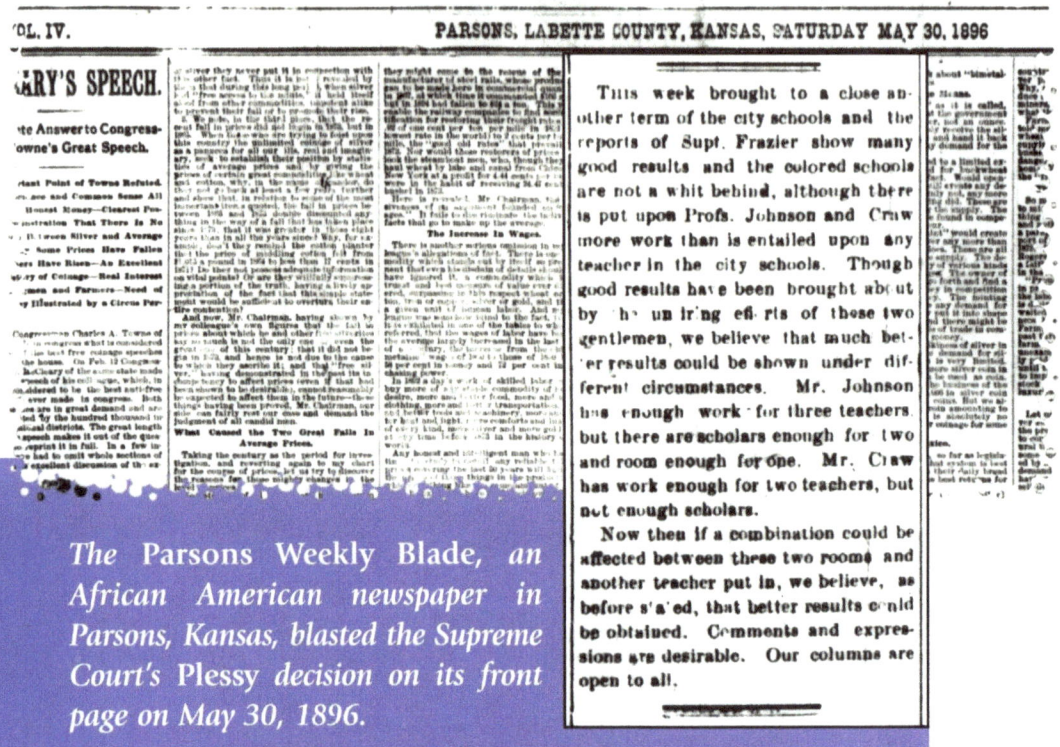

The Parsons Weekly Blade, an African American newspaper in Parsons, Kansas, blasted the Supreme Court's *Plessy* decision on its front page on May 30, 1896.

MEDIA REACTION

The decision of the Court did not generate widespread news. Although the black press covered it extensively, it was generally treated with indifference. Only a handful of mainstream newspapers reported the decision, and they did so without offering an analysis. For example, the *New York Times* carried the decision in its regular railway column. Others ignored it altogether. Those newspapers that offered an opinion tended to criticize the decision.

The Decision

The *New Orleans Times-Picayune* endorsed the ruling. In an editorial entitled "Equality, but Not Socialism," the paper cheered the decision for upholding a distinction between "equality of rights" and community of rights. It reasoned that "otherwise, if all rights were common as well as equal, there would be practically no such thing as private property, private life or social distinctions," which was a recipe for "absolute socialism."

At the other end of the spectrum, the *Parsons Weekly Blade*, a black newspaper in Parsons, Kansas, blasted the majority for having "wantonly disgraced . . . the highest tribunal" of the land. It added that if the Louisiana law could be declared constitutional, "then it is time to make null and void all that tail end of the Constitution; for it is certain that under such circumstances it is of no earthly use." A less strident criticism came from the *Democrat and Chronicle* of Rochester, New York, in an editorial that labeled the decision "strange" and said that it would be "received by thoughtful and fair-minded people with regret."

The Aftermath

For Homer Plessy, the decision meant that the trial that was halted in 1892 would finally take place. On January 11, 1897, four and a half years after he was arrested for sitting in the wrong car, Plessy pleaded guilty to violating the Separate Car Act, paid the $25 fine, and disappeared into obscurity. Louisiana's insistence on trying Plessy after all that time only hinted at the fanaticism with which the South would apply the "separate but equal" principle.

While it is unfair to say that the *Plessy v. Ferguson* decision established "separate but equal" laws, the ruling gave southern states constitutional cover to enact more Jim Crow regulations. "Separate but equal" soon extended to other areas of public life, such as public schools, restaurants, restrooms, community pools, and even water coolers, and the

The Aftermath

This is an arrest warrant for Homer Plessy that was issued in September 1896, four months after the Supreme Court ruled that Louisiana's Separate Car Act was constitutional. Now that his legal fight was over, he had to face punishment for his original crime.

pretense of equality of accommodations was quickly dropped. Public amenities set aside for blacks were obviously far inferior to, fewer than, and farther between those reserved for whites—if they were provided at all. African Americans who dared to use anything that was for "whites only" risked public humiliation (if they were lucky), a beating, or even death.

Segregation became so widespread in the South that it tracked residents from births in separate hospitals to burials in separate cemeteries. The result was the restoration of a caste system in the South that sought to humble African Americans through inferior education, substandard health care, inadequate public

Plessy v. Ferguson

TIMELINE

1619 Slavery begins in the United States when African slaves are brought to Jamestown, Virginia, and sold to plantation owners.

1857 The United States Supreme Court upholds slavery and denies citizenship to all African Americans, free and enslaved, in *Dred Scott v. Sanford*.

1861–1865 The American Civil War is fought between the North and the South.

March 7, 1862 Homer Plessy is born in New Orleans, Louisiana.

1863 President Abraham Lincoln issues the Emancipation Proclamation.

1865 Mississippi passes the first black code limiting the rights of African Americans. The Thirteenth Amendment abolishes slavery. The Ku Klux Klan is founded.

1866 Congress passes the Civil Rights Act.

1867 Radical Reconstruction begins.

1868 The Fourteenth Amendment grants citizenship and certain civil rights to African Americans.

1870 The Fifteenth Amendment gives African American males the right to vote.

The Aftermath

1877 Reconstruction ends.

1887 Homer Plessy marries Louise Bourdenave.

1890 Louisiana passes the Separate Car Act.

1891 The Citizens' Committee is formed.

1892 Homer Plessy is arrested in New Orleans for attempting to ride in a "white" car. Judge Ferguson upholds charges against Plessy.

1893 The Louisiana Supreme Court upholds Ferguson's ruling against Plessy.

1896 The U.S. Supreme Court upholds the constitutionality of Louisiana's Separate Car Act in the *Plessy v. Ferguson* decision.

1897 Plessy pleads guilty to breaking the Separate Car Act and is fined $25.

1909 The National Association for the Advancement of Colored People (NAACP) is founded to challenge segregation.

1925 Homer Plessy dies in Louisiana.

1954 "Separate but equal" is ruled to be unconstitutional in the Supreme Court case *Brown v. Board of Education*.

Plessy v. Ferguson

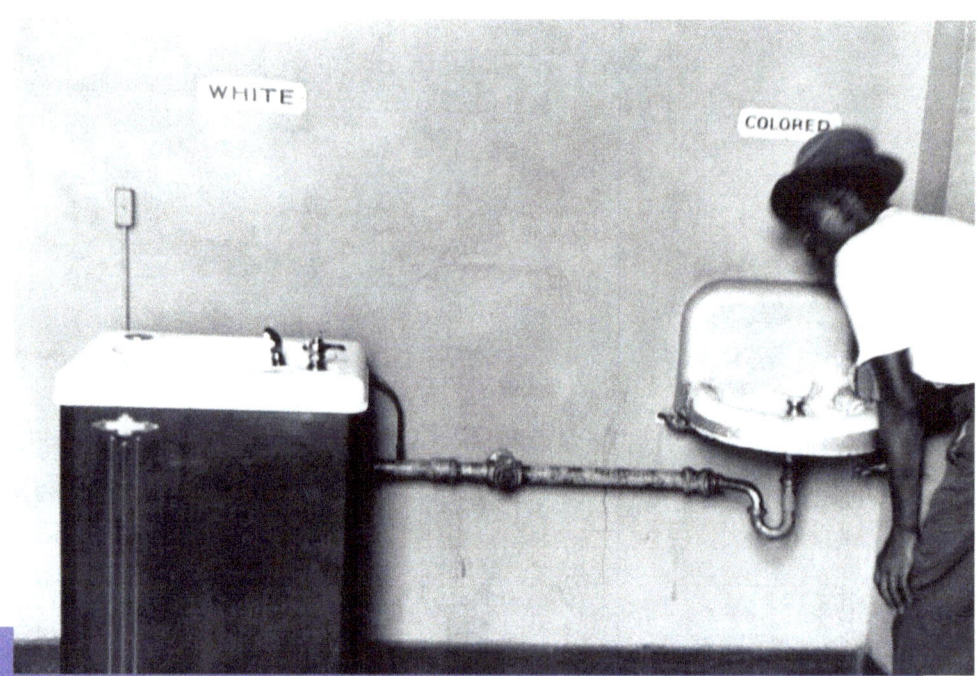

An African American man drinks from a segregated water fountain in North Carolina in 1950. The photograph clearly shows the "colored" fountain to be inferior to the "white" fountain and provides an example of how little attention was paid to the "equal" side of the Supreme Court's "separate but equal" doctrine.

services, and the myriad little insults and put-downs that served as a reminder for them to know their place. In many quarters, even the voting rights of African Americans came under attack.

The "separate but equal" doctrine lasted until it was overturned in a series of Supreme Court cases in the 1950s, beginning with the landmark case of *Brown v. Board of Education* in 1954.

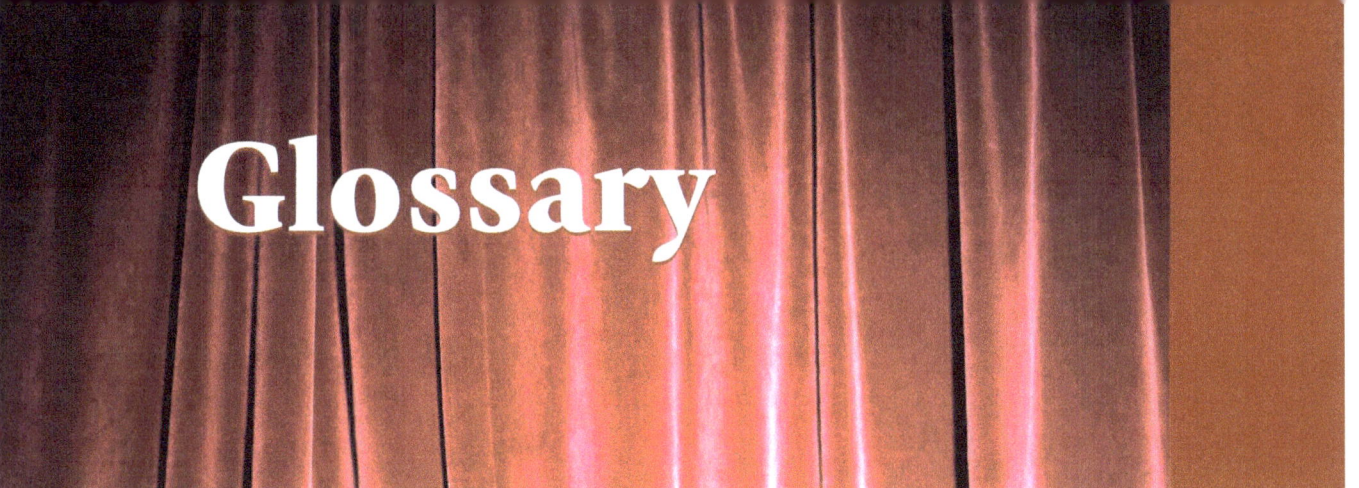

Glossary

abolitionist   A person who supported an end to slavery.

appeal   The transfer of a case to a new or higher court.

black codes   The set of laws passed in the South following the abolition of slavery that sought to control the movement and activities of ex-slaves.

brief   A written legal argument outlining the laws and facts presented by a party to a lawsuit.

carpetbagger   An insulting term for someone from the North who went to the South after the Civil War to take part in the Reconstruction government. They were so called because many of them carried their belongings in carpetbags.

liability   Obligation that comes from the breaking of a law or contract.

petition   A legal request.

plaintiff   The party that institutes a suit in court.

plea   A formal answer to a legal charge in open court or in a written presentation.

Plessy v. Ferguson

secede To break away from an organization.

segregation Separating people of different races, classes, or ethnic groups.

writ of error An order issued by a court of appeals commanding a lower court to send the records of a case to the court of appeals so that the records may be reviewed for alleged errors of law.

writ of prohibition An order issued by a higher court to a lower court that commands it to stop the trial of a case over which it lacks jurisdiction.

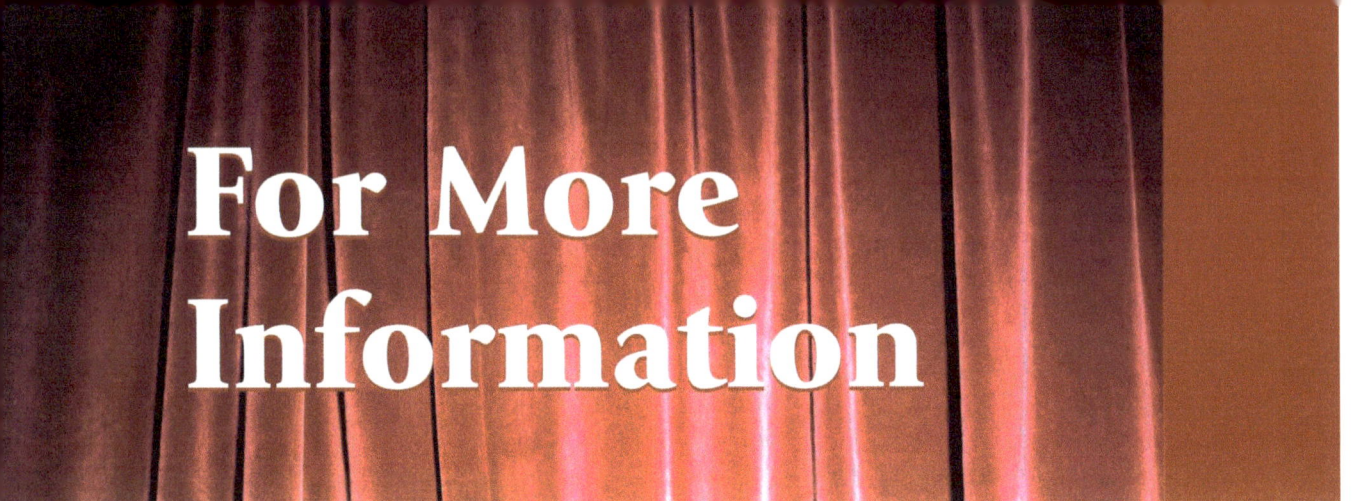

For More Information

National Association for the Advancement of Colored People (NAACP)
4805 Mt. Hope Drive
Baltimore, MD 21215
(877) NAACP-98 (622-2798)
Web site: http://www.naacp.org

U.S. Supreme Court
Public Information Officer
Washington, DC 20543
(888) 293-6498
(202) 512-1530
Web site: http://www.supremecourtus.gov

Web Sites

Due to the changing nature of Internet links, the Rosen Publishing Group, Inc., has developed an online list of Web sites related to the subject of this book. This site is updated regularly. Please use this link to access the list:

http://www.rosenlinks.com/scctps/plfe

For Further Reading

Baker, Ray S. *Following the Color Line: American Citizenship in the Progressive Era*. New York: Harper & Row, 1964.

Fireside, Harvey. *Plessy v. Ferguson*. Berkeley Heights, NJ: Enslow Publishers, Inc., 1997.

Foner, Eric. *A Short History of Reconstruction*. New York: HarperCollins, 1990.

Foner, Eric, and Olivia Mahoney. *America's Reconstruction: People and Politics After the Civil War*. Chicago: Chicago University Press, 1994.

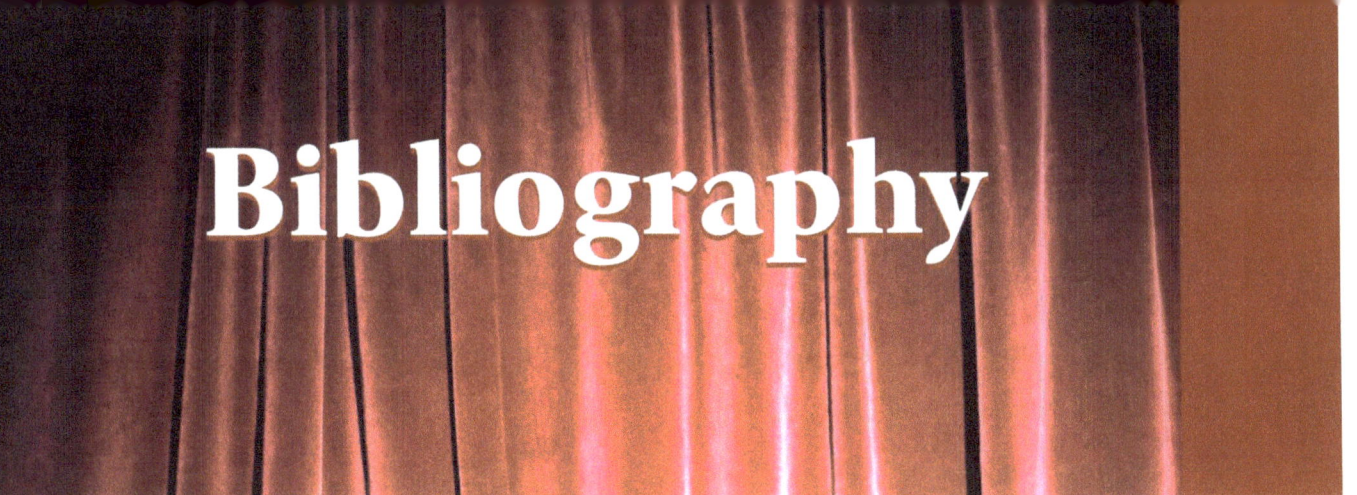

Bibliography

Edwards III, George C., Martin P. Wattenberg, and Robert L. Lineberry. *Government in America: People, Politics, and Policy.* New York: HarperCollins, 1997.

Fireside, Harvey. *Plessy v. Ferguson.* Berkeley Heights, NJ: Enslow Publishers, Inc., 1997.

Lofgren, Charles A. *The Plessy Case: A Legal-Historical Interpretation.* New York: Oxford University Press, 1987.

Kluger, Richard. *Simple Justice.* New York: Vintage Books, 1975.

Thomas, Brook, ed. *Plessy v. Ferguson: A Brief History with Documents.* New York: Bedford/St. Martin's, 1997.

Primary Source Image List

Page 5: Photograph of the U.S. Supreme Court Building, Washington, DC.
Page 8: Lithograph, *President Lincoln, Writing the Proclamation of Freedom, January 1, 1863*, after a painting by David G. Blythe. Created in Pittsburgh, Pennsylvania, by Ehrgott, Forbriger, & Co. Kept in the Library of Congress.
Page 10: Photograph of Captain James M. Robertson and his staff in the Civil War. Taken in Brandy Station, Virginia, in 1864. Housed in the Library of Congress.
Page 13: Portrait of Robert DeLarge, Jefferson Long, H. R. Revels, Benjamin Turner, Josiah Walls, Joseph Rainy, and R. Brown Elliot. Lithograph created by Currier & Ives in 1872. Housed in the Library of Congress.
Page 15: Cover page to Louisiana's Separate Car Act of 1890.
Page 18: Advertisement for the East Louisiana Railroad Company, circa 1900. From the Historic New Orleans Collection.
Page 20: Portrait of Daniel F. Desdunes. Housed in the Amistad Research Center, Tulane University.
Page 21: Document *Ex Parte Homer A. Plessy*. From the clerk's office of the Louisiana Supreme Court. Drawn up on November 22, 1892.
Page 25: Portrait of Albion Tourgée. Housed in the Chautauqua County Historical Society, New York.
Page 27: Joint resolution proposing the Thirteenth Amendment. Signed on February 1, 1865.
Page 28: Engraving of an African American being expelled from a train car. Published in the *Illustrated London News* on September 27, 1856. Housed in the Library of Congress.
Page 31: Portrait of slaves freed during the Civil War. Housed in the Schomburg Center for Research in Black Culture, New York Public Library.
Page 35: Photograph of train crew taken in 1887 in New Orleans, Louisiana. From the Historic New Orleans Collection.
Page 36: Obituary of Judge John Howard Ferguson. From the *New Orleans Times-Picayune* of November 13, 1915.
Page 40: Copy of the Supreme Court order affirming the decision in *Plessy v. Ferguson*. Signed on May 18, 1896.
Page 41: Portrait of Justice Henry Billings Brown, photographed in 1906. From the collection of the Supreme Court of the United States.
Page 43: Portrait of Justice John Marshall Harlan, photographed in 1877. Photographed by Matthew Brady. From the collection of the Supreme Court of the United States.
Page 48: Page from the *Parsons Weekly Blade*. From Parsons, Labette County, Kansas. Saturday, May 30, 1896, edition.
Page 51: Arrest warrant for Homer Plessy. Written on September 23, 1896. Housed in the Amistad Research Center, Tulane University.
Page 54: Photograph of man drinking from "colored" water fountain. Taken by Elliott Erwitt in North Carolina in 1950.

Index

A
abolitionists, 9
Adams, Lionel, 18, 20, 34
Amendments
 Fifteenth, 11, 12, 25
 Fourteenth, 11, 12, 20, 25, 28–29, 31, 34, 38, 39, 43, 46
 Tenth, 33–34, 45
 Thirteenth, 9, 11, 12, 20, 25, 28, 34, 39, 43

B
black codes, 11, 14
Bordenave, Louise, 19
Brewer, David Josiah, 45
Brown, Henry Billings, 39–43, 44, 45–46
Brown v. Board of Education, 54

C
carpetbaggers, 12
Citizens' Committee to Test the Constitutionality of the Separate Car Law, 16, 17, 18, 24
civil rights, 11, 12, 25, 32, 37, 44, 47
Civil War, 9–10, 11, 14, 45, 46, 47
Confederates/Confederacy, 9, 10, 11, 12, 47
Congress, 4, 9, 11, 12, 14, 22
Constitution, U.S., 4, 7, 9, 32, 33–34, 42, 44, 45
Cunningham, Milton J., 33, 34, 36

D
Democrats, 9, 13, 14, 46, 47
due process, 29, 30, 35, 46, 47

E
East Louisiana Railroad, 17–18
Emancipation Proclamation, 7, 9
equal protection, 29, 34, 35, 46
Ex Parte Plessy, 23, 34, 35

F
Ferguson, John Howard, 19, 20, 23

Plessy v. Ferguson

Field, Stephen Johnson, 46
freedmen, 10–11, 12, 14, 31
Freedmen's Bureau, 11
Fuller, Melville Weston, 46

G
Gray, Horace, 46

H
Harlan, John Marshall,
    43–44, 47

I
integration, 12

J
Jim Crow laws, 14, 50
Johnson, Andrew, 11
Judiciary Act, 22

K
Ku Klux Klan, 13, 47

L
Lee, Robert E., 10
Lincoln, Abraham, 9, 11, 46
Louisiana, 5, 9, 16, 17, 18, 19,
    47, 50
  arguments before Supreme
    Court for, 34, 37, 38, 39, 42
  and Separate Car Act, 14, 23,
    26–28, 29, 32, 34, 39, 42,
    43, 44, 49

Louisiana Supreme Court, 20,
    23, 34, 35, 38

M
Martinet, Louis, 16
Morse, Alexander Porter, 33, 34,
    37–38

N
New Orleans, 5, 16, 19
North, the, 9, 10, 11, 12,
    41, 46, 47

P
Peckham, Rufus Wheeler, 47
Phillips, Samuel F., 24, 26
Plessy, Homer
  about, 19
  arguments before
    Supreme Court for, 24–32,
    33, 34, 35–36, 38, 39, 42,
    43, 47
  challenging Separate Car Act,
    5–6, 16, 17–20, 50
  first trial, 23, 35, 50
Plessy Case: A Legal-Historical
    Interpretation, The
    (Lofgren), 26, 38
Plessy v. Ferguson
  aftermath of, 50–52
  dissenting opinion, 43–44

Index

Louisiana's arguments, 33–38
media reaction to, 48–49
Plessy's arguments, 24–32
Supreme Court's decision, 39–43
police powers of states, 34, 38, 42
precedents, 25, 33, 38, 46, 47

R
railroads, and segregation, 5, 14–16, 17–18, 20, 35
Reconstruction, 11–13, 14, 25
Republicans, 9, 11, 13, 14, 16

S
segregation, 5–6, 14, 17–18, 20, 35, 41–42, 44, 50–51, 54
"separate but equal," 6, 14, 42, 50, 54
Separate Car Act, 14–16, 23, 28, 29, 30, 32, 34, 37, 39, 42, 43, 44, 49, 50
Shiras, George Jr., 47

slavery, 7–8, 9, 12, 34, 45, 47
abolition of, 9, 10–11, 28
opposition to, 8–9, 46
South, the, 6, 7–8, 9, 11, 12–13, 14, 25, 50–51, 54
Supreme Court, 4–5, 16, 22, 23, 25–26, 31–32, 33, 44, 54
decision in *Plessy*, 6, 39–44
members of, 45–47

T
Tourgée, Albion, 16, 24, 26, 28, 29, 30–32, 36, 38, 42, 45, 47

V
vote, right to, 11, 12, 37, 46, 54

W
Walker, James C., 16, 24, 26, 45
White, Edward Douglas, 47
writ of error, 23
writ of prohibition, 20, 23

Y
Yick Wo v. Hopkins, 42

Plessy v. Ferguson

About the Author

Wayne Anderson is a freelance writer and editor who lives in New York City. A native of Jamaica, he is a former music editor for the *New York Carib News*, the largest Caribbean American newsweekly in the United States, and the author of four books for young adults. A self-described postmodernist, he maintains an intense interest in the stories of "the others" in society. He is currently working on a collection of poems.

Photo Credits

Eagle on back cover and throughout interior © Eyewire; Red curtain throughout interior © Arthur S. Aubry/PhotoDisc; Wood grain on cover and back cover and throughout interior © M. Angelo/Corbis; Cover, pp. 8, 10, 13, 28 © Library of Congress, Prints and Photographs Division; p. 5 © Corbis; p. 15 © State of Louisiana, Secretary of State Division of Archives, Records, and History; pp. 18, 35 courtesy of the Historic New Orleans Collection, Museum/Research Center; pp. 20, 51 courtesy of the Amistad Research Center at Tulane University, New Orleans, Louisiana; p. 21 © Louisiana State Supreme Court Collection (Mss106), Louisiana & Special Collections Department, Earl K. Long Library, University of New Orleans; p. 25 © courtesy of the Chautauqua County Historical Society, Westfield, New York; p. 27 © National Archives and Records Administration; p. 31 © Myron H. Kimball/Gilman Paper Company Collection; p. 36 © Library of Congress, Serial and Government Publications Division; p. 40 © Records of the Supreme Court of the United States, National Archives and Records Administration; p. 41 © Parker Studios/Collection of the Supreme Court of the United States; p. 43 © Matthew Brady/Collection of the Supreme Court of the United States; p. 48 © Kansas State Historical Society, Topeka, Kansas; p. 54 © Elliott Erwitt/Magnum Photos.

Designer: Evelyn Horovicz; Editor: Christine Poolos; Photo Researcher: Amy Feinberg

www.ingramcontent.com/pod-product-compliance
Lightning Source LLC
Chambersburg PA
CBHW041116070526
44584CB00002B/182